I Shall

Be

Released

A Book of Poetry
By

Jerimiah Whitehead

I Shall Be Released: A Book of Poetry
© 2022 Jerimiah Whitehead

Published by Blu Fountain Streams Publications, LLC.
Flint, MI 48507

The ideas and content of this publication are from the point of view and experiences of the author and does not expressly reflect the views and opinions of the publisher.

Song/Lyric Excerpts: Row, Row, Row Your Boat
Original Author: Eliphalet Oram Lyte, 1852
Parts and lines of lyrics are used for poet expression.

Cover Design: Niki Ferguson
Cover Art Illustration: Jayla Dunlap

ISBN: 979-8-9858174-2-3

Printed in the United States
For Worldwide Production

Dedication

To my family, especially my parents; my siblings, and my nieces and nephews both born and unborn, no one equates to you. I've never loved another human as much as I love you. You really are the best medicine. I'm going to make it through this storm because I have you. I get my strength from you now, then, and always. There are no words that exist that'll completely explain how much I appreciate your place in my heart. We're all we got if you love me like I know you do. Do what makes you happy and be released from whatever's holding you back.

To my Black Brady bunch family, especially the council: I've dreamt of the type of adult I'd be, and with you, I'm him. I can't thank you enough for being you and allowing a judgment free space for me to explore me. We've fought, but no matter how much I pushed you away, you stayed. Your unyielding love is why I'm grateful to have you in my life. You pass the vibe check every time. You quench the thirst of my true self. That's the greatest gift you have ever given me. You are more than a friend, always have been. You are family.

To Prodigy: Thank you for inspiration and mentorship. Your encouragement has led me to this place. A cure for writer's block.

Table of Contents

* * *

Released......................................109

1. Sentencing

To be in the realm of you.
With you is the wildest dream for nights.
I've screamed within the shadows.
You chase my darkest cry.
You stepped on my forceless signals.
You dance....
You hide....
It scares you.
Alerts you.
It is so sad watching you play with my emotions.
But now...
You could put a face to the shadow.
I can dance and hide with you.
Call for you.
You'll actually hear me this time.
You now know I'm alive and I feel seen.
I finally get to wake up from my dream
and feel like I'm still dreaming.
To be amazed with the accuracy of envisioning my
reality.
I feel good...
Like damn good right now.
This must be what the sun feels like.

Hi! My name is Jerimiah.
I traded in pistols for poems.
I prefer you give me a nickname
that no one but you call me.
When I was in pre-K,
my favorite color was pink.
It was pretty and it made me feel happy.
A little boy let me know it was wrong.
Told me to try red instead.
I preferred pink.
So…
I hid it until pink turned to blue.
So did I.
I really miss who I was
before I let this realm proselytize me.

Take me to your heart. You are the intensifying spark to ignite me to live again. I've been dead inside. With your love and God's help, that can surely come to an end. Ain't I rich? You're real and so enticing in every way. Consistently genuine and pure, even when I push you away. You make me feel again. Yeah, I often deny this but baby I'm hooked. I'd be lying if I said that this situation doesn't have me shook.

See I've bailed out on love's foolish game because it seemed the only ones participating are those who use its name in vain. Too many L's, not enough wins. Lately it's been you riding the wave of my frustration as I'm drowning in the depths of your sins. If they ask you, tell them that we're just good friends but you're different. You don't trigger red flags but unfortunately give reminders and clues. Telling me that if I take this any further, I'm risking going to a place I fought so desperately hard to get away from... am I dumb? That I rather be third wheeling chilling instead of used, lied to and back stabbed.

Nowadays the truth is unspoken. Electric eyes are everywhere to capture the make-believe moments. Loyalty has been broken with the shady ways and the defensive plays all for the recognition. Behold the effects of lack of thinking. But you're different and no matter how many times I go on this little rant, something keeps gnawing at my spirit. Telling me to take the risk and give you a chance. As much as I want to ignore it, I simply can't.

* * *

I feel for you. Don't get me wrong, I just think you don't understand being where I've been.

It can make you disconnected and cold shattered into a million and one pieces because I forced myself to love someone I barely even knew. Take me to your heart and I'll truly be gifted. Embrace my sheered imperfections. My soul will be soothed in an instant. You're different, you're the truth. Truth be told, it'll be an honor to be loved by you!

IV

A writer is a mental painter.
We've manipulated the strings of your heart.
We interpret the language of our soul to our readers.
We're wizards and our pencil is our wand.

Dear Walls

Thank you for keeping my secrets.
For not judging me.
For not laughing when I cry.
Lately, you're the one I trust.

Would you be here if you didn't have to be?
Would you preach to me like the others if you had
the ability to speak?
Would you have walked out on me if you had legs
to leave?
Well, no matter the decision I'm glad you're here.
Keeping me warm, making me feel secure.

They think they know the truth.
They think they know me.
You, of all people, know I'm fighting demons.
Losing sleep.
I'm exhausted when I leave.
Since people don't know, they think I'm lazy.

Some nights I'm like a broken record.
Doing the same thing over and over,
but you continue to listen.
Your drywall is wet with tears.
You're the only one I feel comfortable enough to
cry in front of.
Maybe because I don't have a choice.

Some nights I lose my mind,
but in the dark your eyes are open.
Watch over it wherever it roams.
It's funny, when you're alone,
you're not really alone.
Walls can see.

Walls can hear.
Feel what you feel.

Dear walls…

Over the years you've gently forced me into noticing one significant thing.

You can't hide from yourself.

Old Soul

Let's sit and chill for a minute or two.
It's been centuries and I just need to listen to the
breeze.
For I am an old soul and this ain't my first rodeo.
This go round I'm just going to take it slow.

The earliest memory I have of my father is when his wife came to pick me up. My little brothers on my dad's side were in the car. They were so excited to see me, but I don't remember feeling the same. I was scared, waiting for her to be the evil stepmother. Thankfully she wasn't. I just wanted to see my daddy on the ride to his house.

I remember thinking, *I have a daddy like Dee*, my little brother on my mama's side. I remember trying to memorize landmarks so I could know how to find my daddy if I ever lost him again. Eventually, we parked in front of this white house with black trimming. As we were getting out of the car, my little brother pointed at an upstairs window and yelled, "I see you!" I immediately looked up and didn't see anyone. He said it was our daddy peeking out of his bedroom window.

I went inside and followed Charlotte to their bedroom. I saw my daddy sitting on the edge of his bed in the dark room with no shirt, only shorts. (I currently have no shirt on and shorts) He had just gotten weight loss surgery and had this huge scar down his stomach. Everyone left the room, and it was only him and I. I don't remember saying much. I just wanted to be in that dark room with the window blinds slightly opened, letting in 8pm daylight with him forever.

I think I knew I'd never get that moment again because I savored it. I was over there for the weekend. That was the most time I'd spent with him. He was still recovering from surgery and hardly came out of his room.

This was the first time I felt wanted and rejected at the same time.

Grievance

My heart calls for you every second of the day.
In all my conversations I bring up your name.
You're always on my mind.

What do you do when the one who was once next to
you can only be seen in a memory?
When the person whose hugs soothes your soul
instantly is out of your reach…

Grieve.

Bitterness

I'm done falling in love.
Sometimes you really fall.
Wondering, how did I hit an all-time low?
I'm a flower in the basement,
missing the very sun that helped it grow.

I see something in you but can't put my finger on what it is. Anyway, what can I do to show mad affection to you without coming off so thirsty? I don't want to move too fast. I wanna be friends so there'll be no reason for you to reject me.

Lemme deep stroke you with my thoughts. They're throbbing for a space to emancipate its solution to controversial prompts. You yearn for deep conversations. Trust me, I know it's gonna take more than penetration to get through to you.

After reading this, did I make you smile a little bit? If I didn't, I have no regrets. If this gets read, and there's no reply, don't be a victim of a guilty conscience. I'm a big boy, I'll be alright.

Before I go, let me end it with this... I'm not a man with an ulterior motive. My words are protein, hardly ever unintentional. I'm looking for a dope ass friend who gets me. You know, strictly medicinal. Come sink with me inside a vibe and let time decide what happens next.

Bad Timing

Essence,
you've captured me.

I'm moved by radiant,
rapidly changing leaves.
This separation anxiety,
sometimes gets the best of me.

Because my soul still hasn't accepted the fact that
you, the sun and its origin never stays the same.

I can't keep up.
Every day I fight.
With you, I'm heavenly medicated
with a soul purpose to numb my pain
with a side effect of time flying.

Essence,
if I am ever blessed to get you in my grasp again,
I'll drop everything, follow and never let go.
No force on this earth is greater than my love.

You'll see.

You will see one of these old days.
So will I.

Hopefully,
our revelation will expose itself on the same day.

For it'll be a sane day.

Cause you'll see you missed out on a good thing.
I was too blind to see that I was that good thing.

* * *

I know I said I'll play the fool forever.

But thank God forever is so vague.

Dear dream, don't give up on me, I'm coming. If life was simple, I'd fly to you but I'm sometimes in my lowest valley. Running, jumping hurdles, dodging traps. I wish it was a straight shot, but someone keeps changing the route on the map. I'm not complaining, I know I'm not that far away.

What helps me is assuring myself that when I feel like I'm losing, I'm gaining a better version of you. Wait for me. Anticipate my arrival. You're the only priceless thing I can afford. The one that motivates me. All I want to do is get to you. As soon as I do, I wanna pay it forward. I never plan to go back.

And if it's God... God pulled back on his slingshot to propel me to new heights, new dreams; it starts with you. I trust you to be you. Do you trust me to BE?

Dear dream, don't give up on me. Sometimes, I might get knocked down, but I will overcome every weapon that's formed against me. I won't give up because I'm fighting for a purpose. It's purpose that strengthens the warrior in me. Hell has met its match.

I was chosen to be great, blessed, and majestic. A force without remorse to make hellhounds and demons cringe and turn away. I know who I am. Dream I'm on my way. You'll hear my footsteps. You will be liberated by my embrace. Exonerated from your doubt of time. You're mine. Dream, I trust you to be you. Trust me to BE.

Let Me Go

I want to die spiritually,
but my enablers have me on life-support.
There isn't a language they'll understand.
"Let me go."

I am exposed when light dawns on the lesser side. Shows a view of ultimate potential. See, I live in the idea with the goal of being greater, with a set mind to start within. Like shadows, when you stand flat on the ground, the light shows me much higher.

It is my fate. His will, if you will, to be what you desire. Shadows are sometimes scary, which isn't too odd. We often fear our potential which is why we comfortably hide in the dark. But me, I can't be tamed. My presence is unmatched. See, I got that static shock which is why I feel it's my purpose to electrify bodies with countless pleasure. I call it a seldom gesture hoping to encourage the soul to want much better. My presence is mildly consistent but the memory of me is forever.

I love what I do for you but I'm sorry I can't stay. I try to make this clear, but many are extremely determined to make that law change. You could say I am an addiction of some sort.

Doubt me if you must but we have one night only. That's too soon for love. Feelings will be deeper than lust. I like to think of myself as medication to the flesh. You know, a quick fix in the middle of the day to help get you through the rest. I'm never selfish before my volcano erupts. I'll cause a hurricane in ya pelvis. I'm the wizard in yo city of oz. Cause spells I vanquish. Got you speaking in tongues while listening to the sweet sounds of body language.

Let your pores be a vessel to lead me to the areas that'll make your faucet run. You'll be worn out and tired but rejuvenated when I gently whisper in your ear. I'm not even done. I promise no other feeling is greater. I'll hold you while you're asleep, making love to your mind so you'll think of me in your dreams.

Then when the sun abruptly shines in our eyes, it tells you to wake up and demand I say goodbye. That's why it's best I don't spend the night. Hesitant of course, but I soon must go. My absence gives you a better chance of feeling whole. As I disappear into the dark stormy abyss, my shadow will remind you of the last memory of me. It will birth envy each time the next man ends the night with a kiss. He wasn't me and your body noticed.

POV

When you're hungry for something other than food,
more than food,
no guilty pleasure,
no snack,
not even a crumb will hit the spot.
The spot that is the emptiest.
Sometimes the things we don't want,
the things that don't taste the best,
are the things we need.
Where's that hard pill to swallow?

2. Time

Ray was my best friend. We were polar opposites. I couldn't tell you how we met, but I remember thinking we never would. My trauma made me a people pleaser, but my instinct was to go against the grain. Bring order to chaos. People don't like that. So, it's safe to say I had a confrontation with everyone in my classroom, except Rav. I don't remember him being in class the first day or coming in the middle of the year. I just remember him being there when I needed him.

Arguing was a sport to me and I was the MVP. When anyone felt like they were losing, they'd call me gay. It was the joke that was always funny. The bullet that could penetrate Vibranium. The word that turned the sport into a battlefield I call reality. I'm a lover but always had to fight. The boys found out they couldn't win alone so one day they decided to jump me. I'm sure I provoked them and dared them to do their worst because I don't back down from people I don't love. They rushed towards me, pushed me to the ground and kicked me. I felt nothing. I was amazed at how much they were in sync. The smiles on their faces indicated they were bonding. I found joy in bringing them together.

Ray came and told everyone to back up. He told them, "Come jump me." No one took him up on his offer. My pride wanted me to wonder why they feared him and not me, but I chose to be grateful. We were inseparable from that day on. No one ever questioned his sexuality. He wasn't ashamed to hang around me. I was myself around him and felt normal for once. I still have yet to find a friend like that; to meet a man like that.

Rav was ahead of his time. A hero with no cape. He knew being my friend didn't make him gay. After 4th grade I never saw him again. If you're reading this... if I ever have a kid, I want him or her to be just like you. The boy you saved is now a man and every chance I get I pay it forward.

You were my best friend. The boy that never called me gay. You always had my back and never held it over my head. I pray you never changed. You and I are one in the same. Game recognize game. Man respects man.

For that, I love you Ray Burt.

You've stopped... Stopped singing in the shower. Stopped thinking that one thing was funny. Stopped living. You just stopped and I can't help. It's my fault, isn't it? We all know you'd never admit it. I believe your truth to cope without never really knowing the truth.

Why did you stop? Until you give me an answer, I'll keep believing it's me. Since it's my job to protect you, I have no choice but to beat myself up. I'm not happy mama. This can't possibly be what you want. I promised myself that I wouldn't allow anyone to hurt you. There's two people. I didn't think it would ever be you and me.

I'm begging you to stop stopping your voyage to a happier life so I can stop stomping on my spirit. Seeing you like this already makes me feel broken. Start starving your misery and start feeding your happiness. Forget who it hurts. Lord knows you've been hurt enough. Start administering forgiveness to cure the blame.

Let all the chips fall where they lay and trust that everyone is going to be okay. You're nobody's savior but your own. In all actuality, we all make our own decisions. Start putting yourself first. I live for your happiness and I'm slowly dying. I don't want resentment to crystalize your place in my heart. Don't break the heart you made.

I'm going to push myself out of the nest. If you try to save me this time, I'll ask why you can't do that for yourself. Maybe I gotta be the example. The light at the end of the tunnel. Maybe that's how I can start by paying you back. Think of this as eighteen again. You birthed me, I liberate you. Go your own way. I'll never be too far. Whether you're ready or not... it's time for you to start!

When I said *"Hey"*, I wanted to say, *"God I missed you so much!"* When I texted, *"What are you doing?"* I hoped you say, *"Nothing, but when are we gonna link up?"*

I never got that response. From the old you, I've never gotten a response again. This new you seems a little colder. So now, all I have left from you are memories and a frozen shoulder. Was my *hey* that dry? Trust me, I never meant to come off so nonchalant.

There's so much to say but not enough words. Each day apart weakens our relationship. I thought you were aware of the circumstances when you agreed to befriend someone like me, a gypsy. My intention wasn't to hurt you nor push you away. Looking back, I know it seemed like I left you on the back burner expecting you to stay. However, I left to be a better me and I expected you to wait. Believe me, there is a difference.

Now that so much time has flown by, I guess it's my fault that emotions have been depressingly suppressed. And by the looks of things, my coming back seems to be too big of a pill to digest. Yet I am constantly fighting on a troubled sea, in the middle of a storm for a chance to improve things. Hmm... just like old times, I'm always proving myself.

Here I am. Big and bold, offering my pride cause that's just the exterior. Deep inside without you, I'm disoriented. I'm no longer afraid to admit I miss my old friend, but I understand I have not made things easy. I gave confusing signals. Your actions say you're done, but your eyes say you've never left. I should've arranged a face to face to plead my case. Maybe things would be different. We'll never know, will we?

So, that's all folks. It kills me to say goodbye. I guess I'll see you the day after never.

Just know, I tried!

I saw you last night; you and him. Was he the one that ended my suspicion? Was he the one I called? Who pretended, trying his hardest to convince me you were innocent?

I don't know why you continue to do all this sneaking around. You should've brought him inside. Everyone knows your secret. If it is him, thank him for me. Thank him for killing a piece of me. That very piece that aligns the peace in me and kept it there. He saw me too... when you checked to see if the coast was clear. As you looked to your left, he saw me as I was standing right there peeking through the window. I thought it was obvious I wanted to be seen. Yet when you returned to say goodbye and kissed him, he said nothing.

My mild envy placed images in my head playing so viciously clear. I continuously see you, see me, see you seeing me crying inside. Yet I'm still rooting for you. I can't stop or get through to you. I'm your rerun. The world sees me as a fool, he sees me as an opponent, and I don't know what I think of me because I'm too busy thinking of you. To do anything differently would be tough.

It kills me to believe this is the life you've chosen. I'm patiently waiting for you to cease this phase because it's precious time you're abusing. You say you'd rather be where I am, but unfortunately that lie is getting old. You really think I don't notice that you're hardly ever home. I can't picture myself abandoned and forced to face this big world alone.

I'd miss you too much and flames of depression will chill my soul.

Before you desert me, try hard to remain in love with me. Still, I'll shamelessly come running back. Nothing would stop me. Not heaven, hell, rain, sleet nor snow. I'll be there hoping you notice my efforts. That alone should make you terminate this charade and forget about what's his name. I can assure you; all will be forgiven baby. Just come back home.

Curse Broken

It's really over this time.

My favorite song is *Saving All My Love for You.*
And I found someone to sing it to.
To want to feel a song like that completely is self-condemnation.
He was the string that injected a melancholic symphony in my bloodstream.
I promised that I would *save all my love for him.*

That I'll be here waiting for him whenever he is ready.
It's been 7 years.
I must've broken a mirror moments before we met because I'm thinking clearly now.
For it was just a song and you're dead wrong.
Tomorrow I'm taking back all the love I saved and closing the account.

Love and wisdom, they're like jewels. It may be abundant, but it's also rare. I've walked the sands of the Atlantic. Took pictures in Lake Michigan. Flew across the country to LA looking over the city; only to land and become overwhelmed with gratefulness as I allowed reality to sink in. I told my mama I wish we still had our camcorder. When we were crossing the border to Ontario, the bridge frightened me. I had God on call especially when we got on the boat to see a closer view of Niagara Falls.

Within an instant, my fear was erased when I noticed I was staring at a waterfall. I looked at the crowd to see their reactions. There were immediate smiles. I felt two things then as I feel now: joy and favor. That feeling assured me the future would hold experiences that would exceedingly produce fulfillment. Igniting wisdom to make me happier.

As I am kept bold, as I am free, I am a fiend addicted to memories. Love is all I have to give. It is my riches. No matter the circumstances, I can assure you there's an end to it. Be careful what you ask for in this lucid world. Don't take a lifetime to allow the secrets of your mind to remain unrevealed.

Take pride in what you have, you just might have more than the person you think has it all. Be a hunter of dreams and great opportunities. Become an assassin to fear. I know this because I believe love and wisdom are like jewels. It may be abundant, but it's also rare.

Dreamer

A dreamer is the loneliest soul.
A seed imprisoned in its soil that no one knows
anything about.
A dreamer can only dream alone.

Twenty-Three

Every first of the month
I'll keep hitting you up.
Hoping you'll finally give in to being
what you were always meant to be...
Mine.

The Other Man

I broke up a happy home because I wasn't happy alone.

Never said it was right, but I refuse to claim fault.
I've been longing for the sensation of companionship.
Every second my desperation contracts.
Understand that this has nothing to do with you.

Want my advice?
Pick a man that doesn't check all the boxes on my list.
Who isn't so aristocratic.

He blows the flame away from behind my eyes.
He neutralizes the demon I try to hide.

He's the almost that does count.

Your cup runneth over.
Don't mind me as I fill my cup with the overflow.

Why should you be the only one who's happy
when I feel like I'm the only one who's unaided.

Switch places with me.

You tell me then that everything's going to be okay.
Tell me more about the other fish in the sea,
knowing these are the same fish that fishermen
throw back in the water.
You tell me that you wouldn't do the same.

No, I don't want empathy… just your man.

To say I love him would be a lie.
To want him for myself would be a suicide.

Hey, for what it's worth,
I know that if I told him
he'd had to choose,
he'd break the spell I put on him
and choose you.

Exhibit C - Self Hate

I remember being excited to go to my first school dance. My mama bought me this nice 6 am blue buttoned up, slacks, dress shoes, and this blue pastel tie. When she ironed it for me and laid it across my bed. It felt like Christmas. It was what I'd felt I needed. I pictured everyone from class being instantly impressed with my outfit.

My little sister started getting dressed. She never disappoints. She looks good in everything she wears. I just wanted to stand next to her and not mess up the picture. My little brother started getting ready. He had a black suit and white buttoned up shirt. I hated suits because they made me feel fat. I wanted to be the last to get dressed. To save the best for last.

When my sister walked down the stairs, the family was stunned. They showered her with admiration and compliments. That made me anxious. I could no longer wait. I ran upstairs to the bathroom to put on my clothes. I tied my tie and looked in the mirror and fought back tears. I didn't look how I thought I would. I looked FAT.

The smile I had left this dimension. Everyone could feel it. All I ever wanted was to feel beautiful. To not be the ugly duckling in everyone's group picture. I fought back tears because all I could hear were cameras clicking with high anticipation to have something to brag about. Kids with looks that parents wished their children had. I didn't see that in the mirror. I knew I was going to have to go downstairs and let them down.

My mama found me and asked me what was wrong. I said, "nothing," and walked down those steps to hear the family cheering for me. But it wasn't enough. What I felt was unfixable. Still the women tried and said I looked fine; that I was so handsome. I stood off to the side as my little brother came down and the compliments for him seemed less forced. It made things worse. I wouldn't smile for any picture and sulked in any corner I could find, wishing I could hide or skip the dance. But that wasn't an option.

My Stepdad said, "I should've kept my money instead of buying the ticket." For once in a long time, I agreed with him. Before I went to the homecoming dance my mama kissed me on my forehead, but I was too far gone. Not even a mother's love could reach me.

I went inside trying to make the best of it. My brother and sister were homecoming prince and princess in their class. As the teachers place the crown on their head, I remember thinking... *this what I get for trying to be like them.*

Dear Dad

Dad,
We used to talk for hours.
Now all we do is silently fight.
You always made sure there was a step between us,
until there wasn't a need to try.
Some nights I miss you.
Other nights I resent you just as much.
As I reminisce,
it's been years of that.
When will I be through?

Don't worry,
I'm to blame too.
But I came back after the war,
and you stayed MIA.
You were supposed to be the improvement.
The fulfillment of the empty place in my life.
You made it clear that wasn't your job.
It broke my faith in you.
I think I'm still mad
because you came in my life
and turned one empty place into two.

And it seemed like you didn't even care.

I lost my innocence and became a spook, sitting by the door waiting for my chance to get revenge. I think we *been stopped* being friends.

Some time ago, my "friend" followed me to my sneaky link. It was that day she found out I wasn't a cat lover and would rather bury my bone in another dog's backyard. Needless to say, I wasn't ready for her to unveil my extracurricular activities. We never spoke of what she had seen. No confirmation. No *ah ha*! Nothing. That's when I knew my secret wasn't safe with her.

Spending five years on edge, provoking anyone she may have told to anger; hoping they'll expose her. And just when I considered being wrong, it finally happened. Come to find out, she pillow-talked with her boyfriend who was obviously jealous. My guess is she told him that very night and for five years I was their inside joke, at the mercy of the tip of his tongue. An honorary member of the back of his mind.

My secret was placed inside his glass box waiting for a reason to break the glass and use it as arsenal when there was an emergency. Mind you, he was my friend but low key. An enemy. The kind of dude that'll sell his soul just to have one up on me. I'm not even mad at him because of who reloaded his clip and wrapped it with a bow. My best friend. I guess dating someone like him wasn't enough or just knowing wasn't enough. She had to tell somebody. Maybe she didn't care who it would hurt because we probably were never friends.

That's why it was easy to burn him alive with your heart in his possession. You had to learn the hard way. I'm not the only one with a secret. I'll be the whistleblower blowing up this false foundation. Stand tall before it as our twin towers I thought were twin flames burn to the ground. Who knew love was so flammable?

See I didn't have to lie for five years, I did it in your face. That's the difference between you and me. Call me the bone collector, cause you're just a corpse who has yet to be laid to rest. Now, depart from me. Loving you has been a false reality for both parties. Consider this your eulogy.

By the way, you left your scarf at my house. I'm going to keep it. Sometimes I wear it even though I don't need it. It reminds me of our days at EMU before you betrayed me. Damn you for messing up a good thing.

I think I mean thank you for setting me free. One day I'll say it more convincingly.

If I was your woman, would that make you happy?
If I was your woman, would you finally tell me that
you love me?
Would you slow dance with me?
Let me eat off your plate?

Would you no longer be ashamed
to light up when someone mentions my name?

Well tell me this…
If I was a woman, would I even be your woman?
Or would you continue to play games?
Perhaps this is all in my head.
Nah, I'm no fool.
You touch me too seductively.
You hide inside my little bubble too comfortably.
And even though we've never kissed,
if you used a UV light,
it'll reveal your lips print all over me.

If I was your man…
My bad you don't roll like that.
To be yourself is easier said than done.
It's a must if you want to roll with me.

Permission to speak candidly?
That was rhetorical.
See…
I will never be your woman.
You could never be my man,
because my man wouldn't want me to be his
woman!

Forbidden Fruit

I can't be mad at Eve.
I too tasted the fruit of good and evil.
I, too, was heavily persuaded to take a bite.
My cousin touched me.
He persuaded me.
He picked me, lured me, freed me.
Then left me in the sight of God to be judged alone.

Dealt with.
Changed.
Made fun of.
Exiled.
The butt of everyone's jokes.
Studied and beaten up.

When did God start to look like people I knew?
Wasn't God supposed to keep me safe?
God, you put the damn tree there and looked away.
The minute I tasted the fruit, that's when you want
to clock back in and intervene.
You punished me as if it were my fault, I should've
said no.
It happens to everyone; I just embraced it.

God said…
Mom said…
Therapist said…
I said nothing.
Like Eve, I said nothing.

Where did the snake go?
So, he gets to stay in the garden?
What's a little boy to do but survive?
To just obey, so the scary snake can go away.

* * *

Now, all I can think about is the forbidden fruit, trying to chase the first taste again.
To eat it on my terms to make the choice God said I had.

Granny, must you cuss so much?
Oh, I don't mind it. It's fun to see.
My God... you're so funny.
Don't hold your tongue.
You can be yourself around me.
I love it when you are around me.

We were like the best of friends.
Waking up, talking on the phone.
Gossiping midday.
Screaming at the T.V.
Watching WWE.
To us, falling asleep to old westerns,
then repeat.

Life was full.
It was simple, serene, and eventful.
Grandma, I'd stay at your beauty shop
all day with you if I'd have to.
I'm never bored when I'm around you.
Especially if you knew what I went through without
you.
The snake came when you two weren't paying
attention.
But I never blamed you.

Thank you for being a friend my forever
golden girl Essie Mae.
I'll never forget how much.
You and grandma meant the world to me.
My eyes still light up when I see you.
I love you two
because you always came to my rescue.
Even when they begged you not to.

* * *

I had a dog. Her name was precious. She was a Pitbull and I loved her. She'd stand on two legs and rest her front paws on my waist. She was never potty trained. Cleaning up after her was the worst. I petitioned for her to leave a couple of times. I didn't know I loved her. I thought it was weird for humans to love animals just as deep as you would another human.

When she had puppies, she was so depressed I could feel it. Even though she did what she needed to do as a mother she hated motherhood. We housed her and her puppies in a room we called an attic, but it wasn't. It was just an additional room in my brothers and my closet. My parents put a baby gate to separate the room from the closet. Some days when everyone in the house was doing their own thing, I'd go in the closet, call her to me. She'd unlatch from her puppies and jump over the baby gate and just sit with me. My back against the wall and her in my arms we'd just sit.

Time stopped for us. We both were unhappy and felt imprisoned by the ones we loved, hating the job we were assigned. We sat there only letting in what natural light found us from the opened closet door. I knew then that I loved her. She was more than just a dog but arguably, a sister.

Three years later, my friend came to school crying over her cat. I remember being embarrassed for her, thinking I'd never cry over an animal. A week later Precious died and sadness came over me without my consent. I cried harder than my friend. I grieved for weeks and cried on my mother's lap. I told

* * *

myself I'll never cry for a pet, but for a best friend...

3. Visitation

I wish there was a softhearted sugary sweet way to say, "I don't love you anymore." I wish I could tell you when I stopped but there isn't. You deserve to know the truth. All at once it came down to me choosing happiness or you. Believe it or not, it wasn't an easy decision. I can't help but ask, were there things that you forgot to mention? Do you know where our love went? What good are memories if there's a chance we may forget? What good is poetry if it lacks truth?

I have grown allergic to the ingredients in the makings of you. I fell in love with your imperfections and became disgusted by your beauty. It wasn't long before my brain rang the alarm. Opening my eyes only to see I was blinded by your way with words. I was your wings, and you became my anchor, pulling me deeper in the trenches of your codependency. It held me captive in your dungeon you call a heart. I tried to throw scenarios to urge you to let me go and you just ran from the truth. That turned my sympathy into anger.

I took this ride. It was my choice just like it was my choice to leave. Truth be told, both choices were influenced by you. I stayed on for the ups and downs but grew tired of the loops. When I wanted out, you became out of control. I guess the only way you thought you could make things right was by turning the tables. Insisting I made you feel like you weren't good enough.

News flash! You've always been good enough. It's just the chemistry wasn't visible enough. The love wasn't strong enough. You would've noticed had you not come on so tough. I felt entangled in your trauma responses and needed some space. Yet I still fought to keep our love from fading. You jumped in the ring too late. I know this hurts and my change of heart is the reason but in love's eyes I have not committed treason.

I'm not going to be a coward. I'm not going to lead you on or cheat to avoid admitting I don't love you anymore. Like a heart needs to beat, the truth needs to be spoken. It'll do us both some good by telling you this and expelling it from my chest. Just wish there was a softhearted sugary sweet way to say it.

Collaboration

Did you know, composer, that this will be the first and last time you compose a song with me? I'm so high on the highest floor creating vibes for life. Sadly, I don't wanna change your status or prefix. No, I don't wanna make a remix. Let me be your single that goes #1. Become a classic that generations get lifted from our lyrics. Your kiss is always on key. Surprisingly, I vibe with you, but we're in two dimensions.

There are two distinctively different noises of traffic as we're looking out the same window. I love our collaboration. You always know how to release my aggravation. Oh no, I'm not staying. I'm just waiting on my Uber. How can I drive myself home when I'm lit off the taste of you? Tell everyone you're an edible. I'm too receptive to your suggestions. With you, my sacral chakra ain't resting, and I'm okay with that.

You got me feeling so vulnerable. Let me get out of this studio. I'll be birthing feelings, igniting the yearn to fulfill secret fantasies. Passion is filling the room. It's a mood. It's a trap but let me handle the beat. Cliff notes steam my hormones while this whore moans. Sorry, not sorry; let's make love this time. I can reorder a new ride and we'll do it on top of sheet music and poems. It'll make us feel like old money.

It brings a whole new meaning to the command *talk dirty to me.* You give me acoustic fever. Your voice turns my mind into an amphitheater. How do you do that? Make my soul quiver in your chivalry. I thank

God every day for this delivery. Live in me as I dwell in you, caught in the moment baby. I think I'm in love with....

Ding. There goes my Uber. There's my queue to leave. Composer, we made history. Can't wait to tell my friends how you became my favorite song in my discography. Ciao.

If you can't tell someone your worst qualities, it means to some degree you lack self-awareness.

I sometimes use my charisma to disengage the security system that is implemented to protect your heart, then I knock on the wall you built, appearing to be harmless and easy to love.

You'll invite me in as if you really had a choice. I chose you because you needed me. I'm going to try to fix you, love you, listen, and give advice. Build you up until I become sacred to you and your debt to me becomes priceless.

I am your friend until the end or when I have no more use for you.

I do have terms:

Be vulnerable around me at least four times a week. Tell me your secrets to ensure you'll never turn on me.

Sign your name on the dotted line

....

Part 2

There's going to be days where I go places that you can't.

I'll be right next to you but the farthest from you.

Your dearly departed loved ones would be much closer to your grasp than me.

Sometimes I don't come back until you think I never will. You'll never understand why.

Please accept it and don't leave or reciprocate that energy.

I can dish it but if I love you, I can't take it.

I am the sun.

I will brighten up your day and burn you if you get too close.

I wanna fall in love, but I don't want to do the work.

Which is why I don't have no man because there's not enough oxygen for two in my comfort zone.

I keep tabs on everything you do to me.

Never know when I might need it to win an argument.

I tell myself mean things and I won't shut up until I believe it.

I refute every compliment you give me and repeat every insult you told me in my head.

I lack boundaries, so the minute I can't take any more of you overstepping the line you didn't know was there, I'll ghost you.

I exploit my sadness because I feel it was never acknowledged growing up because boys are not supposed to cry.

I'm always scared.

I'm always alone.

I'm never seen.

So, I make people feel confident, supported, and comfortable with being themselves, so they'd feel obligated to do the same in return.

They never do.

I depreciate when I look for validation and acceptance from others.

Part 3

I am owed a higher quality of life.
It's time for a metamorphosis.
I call upon myself to come and save me.
I'll be in the furnace.
Please hurry!

Melanated

Once upon a time there was love coated in melanin.
And…
It walked past me and liberated me.
So much that I became overwhelmed.
What a gem in Ethiopian mud.
I called its bluff, and it showed me.
Told me.
Scolded me.
Taught me to never do that again.

I'm a friend of the melanin.
She told me if I was kissed by the sun and survived,
we could be together.
And so it was.
When I was a kid, people teased me.
Said the sun kissed me too much.
But now, I don't think I have kissed enough.

Drunk texting you gives me a reason to be honest. You got me on YouTube listening to instrumentals, making songs about you. I know I'm gonna regret this, but I'm feeling you and I don't know how to say it face to face. So, I chose to wait until I'm believably drunk. I know what I'm doing, and I know that you're up. According to Messenger and Instagram, you were. I wasn't stalking, it's just the big ass green dot ain't hard to miss.

I'm talking too much ain't I? Just a side effect...This is becoming too long.

Don't make me take the MTA back to the friend zone. You give me a 90s aesthetic and I'm an old Skool kind of guy. Even though we're texting, I'm requesting to be your *Computer Love*, so I can *Zap* you with feelings for me. I'll know the job is done when your heart says, "Roger that!" because *I Wanna be Your Man.*

You were my soulmate, but to the world I called you my best friend. You were never in the friend zone or got friend zoned. I was scared you'd break my heart one day. When we met you said in your intimate relationships, leaving was compelling and you found it hard to stay. So, I took notes and thought I should play it safe. I wanted you from jump. I tried to resist falling in love.

Thank God it was too late. You're too much. Just how I like 'em. Talk too much; too loud when I don't wanna hear it; too quiet when all I wanna do is get to know you. You're too deep; too sexy, and did I mention I got a thing for chocolate? Even when you laugh, it gets too erotic. Forget being exotic baby, you're rare. Now bring your nappy headed ass over here. My Teddy bear. My protector. My coach. My preacher. My doctor. My teacher. My patient. My love in hate and everything in between.

When I say you're my best friend, I don't want everyone to know what I mean. Not because I'm ashamed, but because they'll be jealous to know you spin my world. You're my everything. I'm sorry if I made you feel like you were anything less.

I've had a one-night stand too many times.
It's not even fun anymore.
Same get down.
Same lines.
Different reactions.
But eventually…
The same results.
The thrill is gone when my drive is high.
I'm just cruising in the fast lane of my life.

Worth It

Some people cost too much.
That's why you must cut them off.
Dee cost too much.
But I'll pick up a shift for the rest of my days to pay
the bill of loving him!

The Fight to Be Right

The fight to be right has no end.
Nothing classifies as a knockout.
No final round.
Just ongoing.
There is no true winner.
Except if you forfeit.

There's an old saying that everything has a price tag. My grandma would say it all the time.

It's supposed to mean no matter what, everything has a consequence. In most cases, we do things that we end up realizing was not the best thing to do. We realize this from the following consequences. We're surprised by this consequence every time.

Well, this time I knew... Yeah, I knew how this was going to end. That you weren't ever in love. You just needed what I was giving away generously showcasing my desperation in my loneliness. I mean my longing for you. I dressed myself as an easy lick and you took the bait thinking you were being slick. See, I dreamt the outcome the day before you even knew my name. While you thought you were playing me, you failed to notice you were playing by the rules that I made. Read the engraving on the pedestal you sit on.

It says, "Everything has a price tag, King. I simply paid for what I wanted."

Made in desperation.

Pride

I'm proud when I make someone laugh.
I'm proud I beat the odds. When you say I can't,
I say nothing and show you I can.
I'm proud when I practice restraint and it actually
works.
I'm proud when I defend someone.
I'm proud when I pay my bills.
I'm proud when I cook.
I'm proud when I'm no longer scared.
I'm proud when I see things through.
I'm proud when the sex is good.
I'm proud when I set boundaries. I'm proud when I
keep my word.
I'm proud when I win an argument.
I'm proud when I write.
I'm proud when I can be someone's person.
I'm proud when I give advice.
I'm proud when I speak in front of a crowd.

I'm proud when I don't give up. I almost gave up
three times.

- In 9th grade when I was teased for having a
  big butt. They called me booty.
- In college when I surrounded myself with
  friends that were no good for me.
- Earlier this year because I didn't have money
  to pay rent.

I didn't want to be homeless again.
I almost gave up, but I didn't.

I'm proud of that.

I sent you a message that I know you won't respond to. This is my 57th goodbye. Every time it's more pathetic. I know the real goodbye is yet to come and I don't believe it's this one...pathetic.

I mentioned everything but the truth. I hate you because I love you too much. That's why I want you around but drive you away. Hoping you'll demand I pull over and steer us from dis fucking dis'function. I'm just wondering how did we get here?

Wishful thinking and stolen moments can't be the only reason... it's just not normal. With you I'm breathing and suffocating at the same time. I wanna be your friend but I cannot, and I hate us for it.

My magnetic field pulls you in and you don't even try to resist it. The closer you get, you become distant which makes me try to be perfect for you. Torment is what I've been rewarded with cause between God's jealousy and your mockery towards love, I feel like I'm in a boxing ring getting double teamed. I don't know who's hit hurts the most.

I wanna be free so, so, so badly but I cannot let you go. Change it...do something.... piss me off! Cut out your place in my heart and do whatever with it. Matter of fact, gimme back a little bit. I still wanna be your friend, remember? Am I alone in this underground subway of polluted love? Is emotional distancing the only way to purify it?

Text me back...no, call...wait, zoom is cool. Should we have a witness in the room? I told people about us...

I needed someone to talk to. I feel like I've talked to everyone but you. How could I? You packed your shit. Your side of the story. A piece of make believe. Technicality. I was in love enough, crazy, and dumb enough to help load it in your car. Only to hear you say you'll be back. And I fucking believed it!

You walked out like some victim when it's my life that has been a broken washing machine. I've been on this rinse and spin cycle repeatedly, year after year. Giving me the runaround is the bullshit you prescribe to try to dry my never-ending tears...pathetic.

Forget it. I regret loving you this deeply.

Why? Because after all that...still...

I sent you a message that I know you won't respond to. This is my 58th goodbye. Every time, it's more pathetic... I know the real goodbye is yet to come and I don't believe it's this one...

Pathetic.

Demolition

You were once a solid building.
I had to knock you down.
You were beautiful at first.
You're beautiful now.
You don't look the same,
yet I still love you.
Nothing's changed.

Dear AJ

I'm not ready to apologize for anything. I feel when you get older, you will understand why I do the things I do. As hurtful as today might have been, I'm glad you saw that side of me. I'm not proud of it. I'm not bragging. I'm not insensitive but I'm a little boy in a grown man's body and I handle things as such.

Do you wanna be like that? Do you wanna be 23 years old treating people the way I treated you today? I hope the answer is no. If that's the case, you gotta start growing up now. Speak on things that bother you now. Don't let an issue go unsaid. If you do, you'll end up like me and it's not a good look.

I've taught you so many things without actively trying to. Let this be another one. I have so many issues and you triggered them. I feel like a failure. I feel helpless. I feel unappreciated.

You'll never know what it was like growing up with little brothers. I'm not even going to explain it. What I will say is this, I will never stop loving you, and no matter what mama says. I'll understand if you never speak to me again.

I feel like so much of my youth revolved around y'all   that,   I'm   owed   respect.

If that's too much to ask for, then we will continue to have a strain in our relationship.

I'm sitting in front of you. I went to the bathroom twice to put on more cologne.–Made sure my lips weren't crusty so I would be ready the moment you noticed me. Oh, please look up. I'm tired of watching you from the corner of my eye.

Trying to lock eyes with you has to be the hardest thing to do, but I'll do it for you. I can't leave here without at least knowing your name. Just look at me. Feel what I feel. Ask me for directions. Give me a greeting. I'm glued to this chair until you move. You don't know the power you have right now. I want you so badly.

Your aura is screaming my name. I'm just trying to answer to it. How can I say hello when you caught me staring so many times? How can I ask for your number when I don't know if you swing my way? Just be a man and make the first move. Tap me on my shoulder or get my attention. I'll come over and break the ice so I can bathe in the lake of what could   be.

Damn! You're so cute. A quick glance is not enough to savor. I can't be a stranger. Shoot your shot. For you, the game's been fixed. Here's your chance daddy… you won't miss.

I just locked eyes with you and thought you were incredibly beautiful.

Wept

Life loses its pigment.
Tears tint my eyes.
There are still sunny days.
But they're not as bright as they were before I cried
my eyes out.
If I keep this up, I won't need shades.

4. Solitary Confinement

Oops! I did it again. I ran off another man.

He said he was fine with me as I am, flaws and all. That I was enough. He came on to me, begged and pleaded. That was all I needed to be the fish that blessed his hook. But as soon as he snatched me up, it felt like I was entering a room with no exit. Suddenly, I couldn't breathe. I was kicking and screaming for him to release and leave me as he'd found me. Empty in a sea full of fishes more worthy and less of a mess. Why did he pick me?

When I felt like I was down on my luck, running my last mile... look at the breath of life I ran into. I acted uninterested because when you're single, it's easy to escape and love is too scary to stay in. A punchline to a dark joke has been my love story.

If love wasn't a game of Russian roulette moments before he approached me, my arms would've already been open stubbornly to embrace and kiss him. Cinematically frozen in immaculate relief because when I first saw him, he looked at me and relayed to me what he saw. He decoded the messages I sent to him from a shallow whisper inside of me. He translated it verbatim, verbally. I liked that he had seen the hidden side of me and still wanted to stay. But he'll never know because I pushed him away.

When I was sixteen, I used this dating app. I was looking for love. I wanted to prove to that voice in my head that a man could find me attractive while being attracted to him. What was supposed to take weeks, months turned into, "I told you so". Sadly, I'm still looking nine years later. Searching for what I told myself I couldn't have. Searching for something the people around me have too much of. Longing for something. Not someone. Something like confirmation, validation, reparations for all the years of being single. Looking for love in the same wrong place.

For nine years I put my soul on an auction block. Nine years of hooking up, turning one-night stands into medication that I take once a day. Two times if need be. Tell my friends I'm just freaky, knowing damn well I'm not happy having sex. Unsafely risking contracting an STD because I feel like the least God can do is spare me. It seems I won't find anyone to love me. I can't keep thinking like I'm sixteen. Damn, time really flew by. Take the loss. Maybe the voice in your head meant *no more Bio's, no more hookups, no more nudes. Delete your profile and start dating you.*

Someone walked up to me and said, "Be good to you. In your loneliness, it's going to take some time. You're a dope ass person right now but imagine a healed version of you."

Day one. I blame lies and deceit. Because of them I have become the living definition of bittersweet.

Day two. Millions of suggestions but still confused on what to do. Trying to move forward but my heart won't move.

Day three. I'm black and smooth and with this increasing confidence. I might make you drool. What I'm trying to say is I'm accepting and enjoying my new groove. I am compassionate and empathetic beyond measure. It is those profound virtues that I've buried deep in my heart for my soul to treasure. I am always changing yet remaining me.

Day four. Allowing myself to put things in motion. I'm excited because I truly feel I'm growing.

Day five. Satisfied and anxious. What a mix.

Day six. Never gonna be perfect. I try so damn hard to be.

Day seven. New beginnings may result in a painful ending. I'm disguising my worries. My stomach aches but still, it's a risk I want to take.

Day eight. I wanna feel away, but at home. Free, but held. I wanna close my eyes and still see clearly.

Day nine. A raisin in the sun is what I've been. I was getting better as I thought I was dying.

Day ten. Growing apart from someone you love is sometimes too hard to accept. Wishing for lasting relationships can become too much to ask.

Day eleven. I believe I can, and I will.

Day twelve. It's time to say goodbye to self-negligence.

Day thirteen. My mind has become my penthouse suite, living lavishly and make believe. It's time I evict myself and settle into reality, so I can be the man I was created to be.

Day fourteen. I am not my flesh for my flesh wouldn't be itself if it wasn't for me. I'm a spirit and a free spirit I shall be.

Day fifteen. Tired of holding my fucking tongue for people who don't hold theirs for me. You can do a whole lot for someone, and they should be grateful. But not when verbal emotional abuse comes with it.

Day sixteen. In a sentimental mood. Losing and gaining can't determine whether it's balance or weighting.

Day seventeen. Send me wisdom and in return, I'll give you change.

Day eighteen. I wanna live honestly and be honest, but the truth hurts. With lies, there's less to describe versus being left alone in the dirt.

Day nineteen. I got so much discipline. I'm just disobedient and don't like rules. Not even my own. That's dangerous and admirable at the same time.

Day twenty. Yesterday is over. Today is new. Tomorrow isn't promised. Thank God because I still don't know what I'm gonna do.

Day twenty-one. It takes 21 days to break a habit. Thank God I'm free at last. Feeling accomplished and strong. With God on my side, I can take the whole world on.

Day twenty-two. That love train we were supposed to get on... I think we missed it.

Day twenty-three. The final countdown is what counts the most. It's do or die. Sink or be the captain of the fate of your own boat.

Day twenty-four. Seems as though I grow when I feel low.

Day twenty-five. I'm missing love. I feel it's gone. I fear that truth will show that I didn't try my hardest to hold on, let alone cherish it.

* * *

Day twenty-six. Our bodies perish when our spirit is released. Dear flesh, you must remember I am not you. You are a part of me.

Day twenty-seven. Decisions, decisions… What must I do? Where am I to go? Do I take a sail at sea or do I remain sitting here, awaiting rescue from my illusionist cove.

Day twenty-eight. I choose life. I'm gonna make the best of it until I die. I live for growth. To always seek God and wisdom. That's my oath.

Day twenty-nine. Gratefulness is flowing from my heart. I'm choosing myself and leaving relationships with maturity.

Day thirty. Thirty days of passion, resistance, and shame. All it is to me is treasure. Glorifying in His Name. I have favor and I'm grateful!

The nicest thing you ever called me was the B-word. I don't know if it's a good thing or a bad thing. I've been called so many things and if, off rip, you would've asked me, "What is the nicest thing I can say to you?" I would've said something simple like, "I'm beautiful" or "addictive." Tell me you love me, and you can't see life without me.

Yes, you've already said those things. You wrote four poems, texted about eleven heartfelt paragraphs, and left ninety-two voicemails. You never ran out of ingratiating words for me. To be consumed and hoarded in this studio space inside my heart designated for you. I cherished your words like Grammy and Oscar awards. On the highest mantel is where I keep the nicest thing you said to me. The B-word. You could've just said I was smart or at best intelligent. Those words couldn't have possibly communicated entirely deep down what you think of me. So, you found a word that did.

You were on the phone. I was in my dorm. You told me I wasn't like any other guy you'd ever met. You called me *Brilliant*. Nobody has ever said that to me before you. I don't know if it's a bad thing that being brilliant is what I deem the nicest thing you've ever said to me. Either way I love you for it. I forfeit arguments because of it, and you know I'm never wrong. I'll vouch for you even when you are through. Not to enable you, but just to prove to you how far I'll go. From then on you go wherever I go. You dared to love me and in the most pleasant way you're stuck with me and I'm the lucky one.

* * *

I'm brilliant. Full of colors. You and I make the greatest hue. Thank you for not allowing the cat to make your tongue it's prisoner. Thank you for the roses while we were together. Its beauty makes the prick from the thorns that conjured our not so happy ending worth it. Because of your words, our story is still a good read. Here's my confession; sometimes I miss you or just the confidence boosters you gave.

To aid my cravings of you, I go to that crowded studio space in my heart packed with your words. I bathe in it. Pour a double shot of it. Consume it. Grind it. Roll it up and smoke it. Sleep on it. Wake up to it.

And before I leave, I look at my mantle and caress that B-Word. Marveling in the memory of our first rendezvous. In fact, it's what obliges me to ask, "What was the nicest thing I said to you?"

Don't Look for Butterflies

The best relationship advice I'd give myself is don't look for butterflies.

I'm not coming from a bitter place.
Butterflies sweetened the taste of red flags.

If you go looking for butterflies,
you'll never find the love that loves you back.

The kind of love that reciprocates.
The kind of love that gives life,
instead of the love that gives pain.

Every time I had butterflies, I ended up with a stomachache.

I'm Enough

I never wanted to be a woman but if I ever do,
despite what people may think...

I free myself from people's opinions,
good or bad and accept me as I am.

I'm through with trying to fix you.

It only made me realize,
you don't need fixing, I do.

I accept you as you are but...

You must adhere to my boundaries if you want to
be in my life.

You can't change me.
You can't contain me.

If I make you uncomfortable by being me...

Leave.

I am enough.
I am enough.
I am enough.

I want you in my life but if you refuse to see me,
you have to go.

If I have to be alone,
so be it.

The most pivotal moments happen when I'm by
myself.

I stand by me through it all.
The good and the ugly.

You can't control me,
I'm free.

You can't disown me,
I'm free.

You can't win,
I'm free.

See me.
See my wings.
See the rainbow.
See the sun?

Come with me.
Open your mind and dance with me.

If you can't,
come when you can.

If you never do,
it's cool.

Cause,
I am enough.

I wish people would stop thinking that apologizing immediately pays off the debt of their wrong doings.

It is only a down payment and the severity of their fault determines the terms it takes to get back someone's trust and/or love.

If you're unwilling to do whatever it takes to make things right, I don't want it.

In retrospect, I understand and accept the responsibility.

It's up to me to tell you what I need in order to move forward to make it right.

If you did the unfixable, that too is a message I must relay.

I knew I loved you when I held you in my arms, rocked you to sleep and played with you. Got whooped for you. Fought you, ignored you, hurt you. I knew I loved you when you gave me all the love, I'd given you. Back when you sacrificed just as I did. Leaving you has never been easy. Not being able to hold you has felt like a punishment. I know you're grown now, and you don't see things the way I do. Just try to.

When I see you, I still see the baby version of you when you're in pain, so am I. If I could carry you on my back for the rest of my life, you'll never be too heavy to hold. You'll never be out of my grasp little brother's. Little lights of mine, no matter where I go in life. I've already lived my best days with you. I've always hated myself because I wasn't your typical big brother. We never talked about girls... *EW*.

My clothes were too big to pass down to you. I was different, making your experiences different. Everything I did, it fell back on you. I hated that. As a big brother, I knew I had to give you something. I wanted to give you what myself and not many other little brothers had. Love and affection from a man who wanted nothing in return. Hugs and kisses and arms to hold you. You'll never be too old for my love. I failed at so many things, but I know I made it clear that I loved you. I can live with that. I hope that was enough.

I've been telling anyone who'd listen, that you may never be here in human form. If you are, here's what I have to say:

I've always in some ways helped raise a child. I've been the oldest for years until my big sister came. I have been a huge part of my nieces' lives. I worked with kids, and I feel like it's my turn to be loved and nurtured by me. To bathe me, clothe me, raise and teach me things. To spend time with.   To watch grow... *and all of this is bullshit*, but I do want   you.

I want to make sure I'm the best me before meeting you. But I'm scared. I'm scared that if I have you, I'm going to feel like I made a big mistake. Then leave like my father left me. I love you too much to put you through that. What if I did my best and still messed up? I don't think I can handle hearing I failed you.

I lose patience sometimes. One-minute I'm mean, then I'm nice. I'd love you so much, I'd be terrified to lose you. You'll have my life in your hands. I'd be a hamster running on your wheel. My heart would be at your mercy. I just claimed my life back. Would it be fair to give it up to you? I just started loving myself. I don't know if having kids is too soon to think about or not for me. But if I do have you, let's be gentle with each other's hearts... Okay.

* * *

Table for One

I feel fresh air when I'm away from you
and it makes me feel guilty.

I found happiness outside of you
and when I send you my location,
the moment you pull up,
I lost it again.

God, I hate that.

I see now why people are so apprehensive to take
the next step.
To walk through a new door to elevate.
To fly.
To leave.
It's because of just that...
You leave.

You leave the people you promised you would
always be there for.
You leave them to fend for themselves just as you
have been doing.
But it's different when the tables turn and it's you
whose turn it is to experience joy.
Your time slot to enjoy the fruits of your labor.
All you want is for the hungry to come eat with you.

But I can't invite you to place that only has room
for one.
I can't keep choosing you over me.
I can't stay with you anymore.
We know this, but it hurts so bad to leave.

I want the sunshine.

I want the breeze.
I want what's on the other side.
It's inviting me.
I have to go.
I leave myself no choice.
I know you understand.
It doesn't make it hurt any less.
I thought it would.

Lock the door behind me.
I am not coming back.
This house feels like a closet.
I'm through with that.

I'm trying to find a poetic way to articulate this hollowness I'm feeling.
I only end up sounding stupid, so I'll get to the point.
I told myself that I wasn't going to depend on anyone.
I wanted to carry myself through the storm.
It's hard, but I knew it would be.
I can handle it, but the situation doesn't seem handled.
I'M LOSING!
I'm not disciplined.
I'm waiting on luck and miracles.
I don't know how to do anything else.
Surprisingly, I don't want to escape.
I want to fast forward this part of my life because I'm losing.
I hate to lose.
The worst part of the journey is when you feel like you're not moving, each time you take a step.

Vengeance is I says the Lord...respectively I say to thee please hurry. I'm hurting. What do You do when they hurt Your feelings? When they lie to You, beat You down when no one's looking? Build You back up when everyone is around? What do You do when the people You love are jealous of You? Old friends have a disagreement and wish the worst for You?

What do I do when they curse me? Call me out my name, laugh at, tease me, talk about the way I dress or my weight? How can I retaliate without displeasing You? In the past, if someone did something wrong to me, I walked away and everyone around me made me feel weak. I've been taught to fight back with my words, fists and silent treatment make them hurt just as much as I hurt. Risk losing a relationship that'll take a lifetime to retrieve it, if not longer.

Once accomplished, the feeling is rewarding at first but quickly, it uncontrollably fades. Then I look in the mirror. I see my body with their face. It's not fair, I believe in You. There's no doubt in my mind. Sometimes these situations, after an altercation, frustrates me because I feel like You're taking their side.

Someone asked me what happened between me and you? Why didn't we reach the place we were getting to?

I said it's because there was a person who you gave your heart to before there was even a me, and they never gave it back.

Making things one-sided and one-sided love feels heavy when you're the only one who has something to give.

One Last Time

I can't fight it.
His love is just too strong.
Dare we try again?
I'm going to let him back in.
He's home now.
I better tidy up the master bedroom.
Reassign one another a side of the bed.
We're going to try one last time.
We're going to last this time.
Even though we said that last time.

Numb

If only you knew the shit I go through when preparing to give myself to you. Why crucify me if I don't feel like it? I wish there was another way to satisfy you. Another way to make it official... I'm not scared to do the deed; I just don't feel like it.

If only I could conjure up enough strength to say no. My mouth stays closed cause I don't feel like explaining something you don't even try to understand. So, to avoid an argument, I unwillingly, willfully go through with it. telling myself if this turns into love then it'll all be worth it. But if it does not, I'll have to live with it.

I'm what you call vulnerable without any resistance. Take from me what you find valuable and be nourished. Even though you only care about your needs, if compassion should take over your heart don't worry about me. Because as you're seizing my treasure for pleasure, I don't feel a thing. I've become numb. *You make it sound like rape.* That's what it feels like.

Sixty-Five

Lay on my chest and let my heart say the things I can't articulate.

Blind Leading the Blind

I look for answers from people who have the same
question as me.
It feels like going to a water show thirsty.

Row, row, row your boat gently down the stream…

They sing this song to you to pre-warn you. To tell you to not get too comfortable. *Life is but a dream.* What you came with is what you'll leave with. What if there's no seeing you in the great awakening? What if there's only coincidental meetings throughout our eternal path. Does this mean there's no one to really hold on to? No one that's really for keeps.

Are people just things found in a dream?

Isn't it annoying when you find a wad of cash and put it in your pocket and hope to have it when you're done dreaming. Only to wake up and look for it and it's not there.

Could it be that you're equivalent to a lifeless thing and this bond we have is just make believe? Is it something I think I need, a lesson, some sort of training? Am I rowing through simulated love to stimulate me? What if what's real is in the eye of the beholder? Please be universally real. I want to think of you and be relieved to have you physically when we cross over from this stream.

Would I even feel pain if I don't remember you? Would I be saddened but not know the reason? Is that my mission now…to find you? Just to be loved by you once again?

I have so many questions, but I won't be misdirected by trying to always make sense of things. Though I can't imagine an existence without you, I'd never try to cheat the stream.

All I can do is love you gently throughout my life. One day, merrily I'd wake as my body and soul disengage and patiently wait until the next dream to do it all over again.

You see, that's how I love. That's why I'm so apprehensive when meeting someone new. If we got to know each other, one day there'll be no scenic view that can rival the sight of you.

Unpopular opinion, sometimes there's no pleasure in knowing we have to trust that God knows what He's doing. That letting go is our best shot at holding on.

There's no happy ending. Things would have to end for there to be.

Love knows no bounds. We'll find each other again, but how? That's the question I can't answer. Nothing to be sad about. People you love never truly leave. To love hard is not a liability.

I've been sent to remind you to just...

Row, row, row your boat gently down the stream

merrily

Life is more than just a love story between flesh and soul.

merrily

Death is nothing to fear.

Merrily, merrily, merrily

Life is but a dream.

And when I wake, I get to see you again.

Scratch My Itch

I lift my window and ask the wind about you.
I tell it to hug and kiss you.

If it's been windy lately,
blame my million thoughts of you.
Stand still in my mind.
I insist on not resisting you.
In you is where I want to be.

As I cup your face in the palm of my hand.
Melt and await a kiss on the forehead.
Our love can solidify the sea.

I want to foreplay with your soul.
Be deemed memorable by your subconscious.
So, when you're far away,
A lucid dream can be our FaceTime.

Just hurry back home to me.
Kiss me in the spots that only you have seen.
I can taste the buildup.
I'm not safe.

Anyone could walk through this door,
and my eyes will give them your face.

Have them scratch my itch.
Is your touch laced with dopamine?

Never let go of your hold on me.
My neck can feel your pulse through your fingertips
when you choke me.

Too many flashbacks are torturing.

• • •

When you are away,
You are a fairytale.
And I'm in this castle,
guarded with fire breathing dragons.

Conversing with the wind,
Waiting for you to save me.
Turn this tale into the real thing.

A flame that flickered but was never lit.
A flame that was already blown before I even made
a wish.
There's no heat between you and me.
The audacity to blow smoke and still be freezing.
How is it I'm a pyromaniac who has yet to be
wooed by your flame?

And look at you now...
Hurt don't last always.
You're so strong.
A lot of people remain stuck.
A lot of people can't make it through a heartbreak
but look at you.

Creating this book,
I've had multiple dry cries.
The tears have been absorbed in the words.
Wring it out and be nourished from it.
Feel me deeply.
See me clearly.
Cry with me,
but don't stay sad.
I'm healed.
I'm finally free.
I'm finally me again.

5. Released

That's Why I Love You

Your strength.
Your courage to be disliked.
Your stubbornness.
The fact that you always choose me
when it truly matters.

Your voice.
Your mind.
It's why we're here in the first place.
The details of you are so astonishing.
I never wanted anyone more.

You gotta believe that.
Come here,
I just wanna hold you.
Listen.
I never stopped having faith in you.
You can't self-sabotage me out of your life.
You hear me?
You won't ever have to worry about me leaving you
when it's too hard to love you.
I'll always find something new something about
you worth holding on to.

That's it.
That's what I came here
in this mirror to tell you.

• • •